Dogs

Children's Nature Library

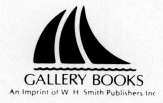

GALLERY BOOKS
An Imprint of W. H. Smith Publishers Inc

Manufactured in Yugoslavia.

8 7 6 5 4 3 2 1

ISBN 0-8317-6461-9

This edition published in 1991 by Gallery Books,
an imprint of W.H. Smith Publishers, Inc., 112
Madison Avenue, New York, New York 10016.

Gallery Books are available for bulk purchase
for sales and promotions and premium use. For
details write or telephone the Manager of
Special Sales, W.H. Smith Publishers, Inc., 112
Madison Avenue, New York, New York 10016;
(212) 532-6600.

Contributing Author: Teri Crawford Jones

Credits:
Animals/Animals: Roger & Donna Aitkenhead:
38; Henry Ausloos: 4, 51; Norvia Behling: 5, 26;
Margot Conte: 10, 11; Jerry Cooke: 22, 23, 60;
Dagmar: 16; Richard Kolar: 20, 29, 31, 45; Jayne
Langdon: 46; Zig Leszczynski: 3, 14, 19, 36; Joe
McDonald: 48, 64; Brian Milne: 6; Oxford
Scientific Films: P.K. Sharpe: 7; Charlie Palek:
49, 58; Robert Pearcy: Front Cover, 1, 21, 22,
24, 25, 26, 28, 30, 32, 39, 42, 46, 52, 53, 56,
57, 59, 62, Back Cover; Maresa Pryor: 33, 35;
Michael & Barbara Reed: 47, 63; Mike & Moppet
Reed: 54, 55; Ralph A. Reinhold: 4, 6, 8, 9, 30,
36, 37, 56, 58; LLT Rhodes: 52; Frank Roche:
38, 61; George Roos: 30; Leonard Lee Rue III:
44; Alfred B. Thomas: 12, 13, 20, 26, 48; Sydney
Thomson: 18; Barbara J. Wright: 28, 44; **Click
The Photo Connection:** Diane Calkins: 34;
Rosemary Shelton: 34; **FPG International:**
Zimmerman: 27; **International Stock
Photography Ltd.:** Bob Firth: 50; Michele &
Tom Grimm: 15; Andre Hote: 18; Robin
Schwartz: 17; Wayne Sproul: 50; Robert Tulin:
40; **Unicorn Stock Photos:** Aneal Vohra: 43.

Table of Contents

Introduction

A wagging tail and a friendly, cold nose—what animal has these features? If you guessed a dog, you're right. Dogs are found all over the world. They come in many shapes and sizes. They are frisky, playful animals that love to be with people.

Introduction

The first dogs may have looked a lot like wolves. They appeared millions of years ago. Since then, dogs have changed into many different breeds. But modern dogs still belong to the same family as wolves. They are also related to coyotes, jackals, and foxes.

A long time ago, dogs moved in with people. Dogs helped people hunt for food and protected their homes. People gave dogs food and a place to sleep. That's how dogs and people became friends. This friendship has lasted over 10,000 years.

Famous Dogs in History

One of the most famous dogs of long ago is the Afghan (AF-gan). Two Afghans might even have been on Noah's ark. Afghans originally came from Egypt. They can run very fast. Kings once used them to hunt antelope. Afghans have long legs and thick, silky hair to keep them warm.

Famous Dogs in History

Irish Wolfhound

The ancient mastiff was a war dog. It fought alongside the Romans and the knights of the Middle Ages. Today this huge, gentle dog is happy to guard its home and family.

Irish wolfhounds hunted wolves with Irish kings and queens. These dogs are nearly three feet tall. They love children and will protect them from all dangers.

Puppies

Baby dogs are called puppies. They are roly-poly,
fat balls of fur. Puppies jump on almost anything
that moves. They yip and chase their own tails.
They tug on toys or chew old shoes. Puppies will
play until they get tired. Then they will drop to
the ground and fall fast asleep. After their nap,
they are up quick as a wink and ready for another
game.

Puppies

Most mother dogs have more than one puppy. Sometimes a mother dog will have as many as 16 puppies. When puppies are born, they are blind and deaf. They drink milk from their mother. After two weeks, their eyes open and they can hear. Puppies grow very quickly, so they need lots of food and rest.

After about four weeks, puppies begin to explore their world. Their mother watches carefully as her puppies sniff and look around. She also shows them what is safe and what is not. She even teaches her puppies how to play. By the time puppies are eight weeks old, they are ready to live away from their mother.

Dog Talk

Even though dogs cannot talk like people do, they have ways to express themselves. When they want to play, they bow down and wag their tails. When they are happy, they may run in circles or want to lick your hand or face. If they are sorry for something they did, they might roll over and show their stomachs or hang their heads.

Abby

Dog Talk

A dog also talks with its tail. Dogs wag their tails when they are happy. When they are afraid, they tuck their tails between their back legs.

Barking, whining, and growling are also dog talk. A bark may say, "Glad to see you" or "Play with me." A growl can be playful or angry. Whining usually means, "I want to be somewhere else"—like having fun outside.

Caring for a Dog

Dogs need good food and fresh water every day. They need room to run and play. They also need a place to sleep that belongs just to them. This could be a comfy blanket in a kitchen corner or a snug doghouse in the backyard. Every dog needs love, too. You should always give your dog lots of hugs and pats to show how much you love your special pet.

Caring for a Dog

When dogs get dirty, you have to give them a bath with a gentle dog soap. You need to stand back when a dog shakes off the water. Otherwise, you may get a bath, too!

Sometimes you have to comb a dog's fur to get the tangles out. This is called grooming. When poodles are groomed, they often get fancy haircuts. They might even get ribbons in their hair.

Training a Dog

Training a dog isn't hard. Only one trainer should work with a dog that is learning new things. At first, dogs should learn to walk on a leash. Then they can learn to sit. Push down gently on a

dog's back end while saying "sit." Do the same when teaching a dog to lie down. First say "sit." Then gently pull the front legs out and down while saying "down."

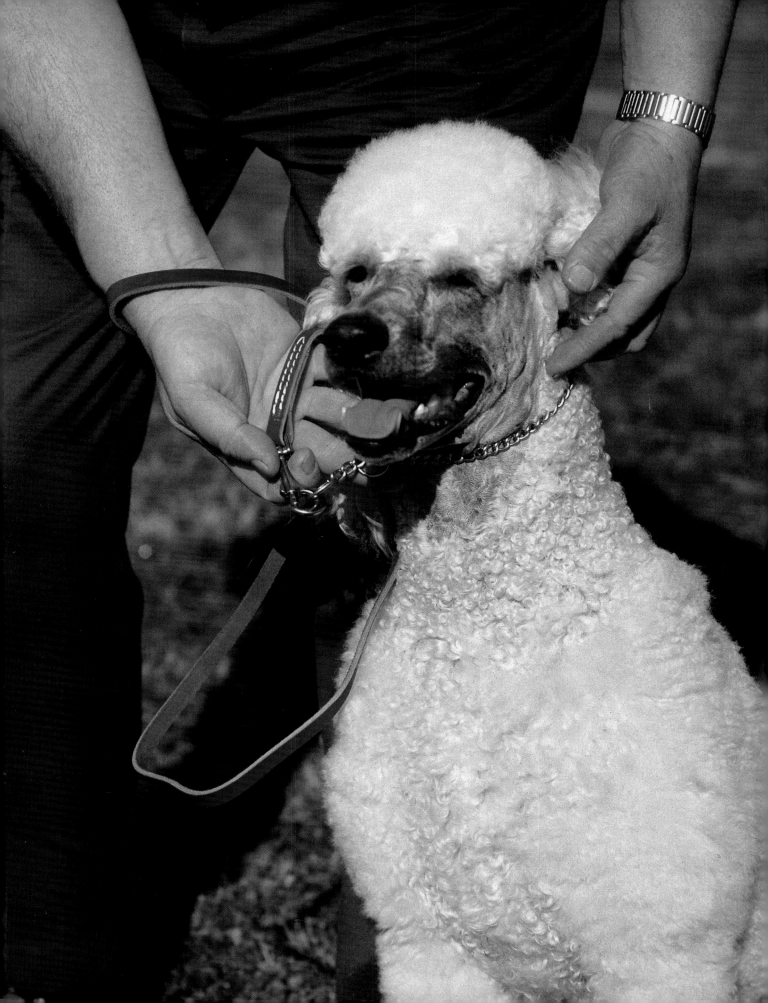

Training a Dog

Smart dogs can be taught to do all kinds of things. They can be taught to roll over or fetch a newspaper or slippers. They can learn to jump over fences and climb ladders. Some dogs can play dead. Little dogs can walk on their back legs.

Give dogs lots of praise when they do something right. They love to hear you say "good dog."

Working Dogs

Border Collie

The black-and-white border collie herds sheep. Around the herd it dashes, barking and snapping at the heels of sheep to keep them together.

The blue-eyed huskies work in teams to pull heavy-loaded sleds across ice and snow. They have thick fur to protect them from the cold wind.

Even though most Dalmatians (dal-MAY-shuhnz) are now pets, they have always been popular as firehouse dogs, too.

Dalmatian

28

Husky ▶

Guard Dogs

spikey

German Shepherd

Doberman Pinscher

Rottweiler

Guard dogs are smart, loyal, brave, and speedy. The German shepherd and the boxer help protect police officers in dangerous places. They can climb stairs and jump through windows. They use their keen noses to search for people, drugs, or bombs. The dog and the officer are close friends and a good team.

Other guard dogs are Doberman pinschers (DO-buhr-muhn PIN-chuhrz) and rottweilers (ROT-WY-luhrz).

Boxer ▶

Helpful Dogs

Many dogs are more than friends or workers.
They are people's eyes and ears. Guide dogs are
trained to lead the blind. Most guide dogs are
German shepherds, Labrador retrievers (LAB-ruh-
DAHR ri-TREE-vuhrz), or boxers. They wear a
harness for a blind person to hold on to. These
dogs lead people safely through the streets. They
know when to stop and when to go forward.

Helpful Dogs

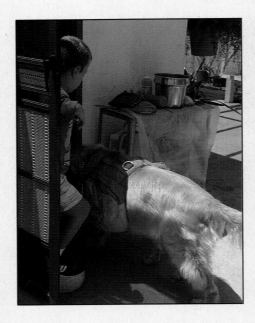 

Dogs are also trained to help deaf people. They let their owners know when someone is at the door or that the phone is ringing.

Other dogs help people in wheelchairs. They pick up or carry things and bring newspapers, clothes, or shoes. Some helpful dogs even visit elderly people in nursing homes. The friendly dogs help these people feel cheerful.

To the Rescue

German Shepherd

Doberman Pinscher

Many dogs rescue people from drowning, find them if they're lost, dig them out of fallen buildings, and pull them away from fires.

A famous rescue dog is the Saint Bernard. This huge and gentle beast has been a welcome sight to people caught in mountain avalanches. Saint Bernards have wonderful noses. They can smell people buried under deep snow.

German shepherds and Dobermans search through fallen buildings after an earthquake. When they find someone, they dig and bark for help.

Saint Bernard ▶

To the Rescue

Newfoundland

The Newfoundland (NYOO-fuhn-dluhnd) can rescue drowning swimmers. This huge, bearlike dog loves water. It has webbed toes and an oily coat for swimming.

The bloodhound can smell the faintest trace of a person's footsteps. These dogs often track people lost in mountains and forests.

Top Performers

Some working dogs are famous. They appear in movies, television shows, commercials, magazine ads, and circuses. They are amazing, funny, cute, and entertaining.

Performing dogs can do all kinds of tricks. Circus dogs jump through hoops, dance on their back legs, ride horses, and balance balls on their noses. Movie and television dogs run, bark, growl, and whine on command. They also play dead, carry things, and swim across rivers.

Top Performers

Chihuahua

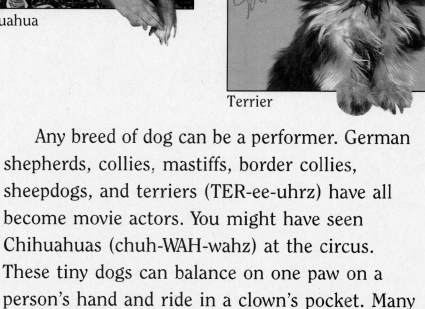

Terrier

Any breed of dog can be a performer. German shepherds, collies, mastiffs, border collies, sheepdogs, and terriers (TER-ee-uhrz) have all become movie actors. You might have seen Chihuahuas (chuh-WAH-wahz) at the circus. These tiny dogs can balance on one paw on a person's hand and ride in a clown's pocket. Many dog stars do not belong to any special breed. They are just dogs that everyone loves to watch.

Sporting Dogs

Pointer

Spaniels (SPAN-yulz), setters, retrievers, and pointers are all sporting dogs. The names of these sporting breeds give some idea of what they do best. A pointer freezes when it smells or hears a rabbit or bird. Its head is straight out and "pointing" to where the animal is. Golden and labrador retrievers leap into ponds, lakes, and swamps to bring back, or retrieve, birds.

Golden Retriever

Golden Retriever ▶

Sporting Dogs

Spaniel

Pointer

Spaniels are also water dogs. They dash into reeds and brush to scare birds into flying. Spaniels have wavy, feathery fur and long silky ears.

A beautiful sporting dog is the Irish setter. Its coppery red fur looks like a new penny. They point, and then drop to the ground and wait. They move only to bring back the hunter's catch.

Popular Pets

Cocker Spaniel

Many dogs were once hunters or guard dogs. Today they are popular family pets.

Golden retrievers were named for their beautiful gold and cream-colored fur. They love to swim and play. Like the retriever, the cocker spaniel (KAHK-uhr SPAN-yuhl) was also once a hunting dog. But families enjoy the cocker for its cheerful, loving ways.

Golden Retriever

Popular Pets

Basset Hound

The sad face of the slow-moving basset
(BAS-uht) hound hides a merry, lively dog that
loves to play with children. The beagle is another
popular hound. It is friendly and very smart.
Many beagles love to play jokes on their owners.

One of the bravest dogs is the Scottish
terrier. It walks about proudly, head high and tail
straight up.

Scottish Terrier

Popular Pets

Poodle

Schnauzer

One of the smartest, most popular dogs is the poodle. It comes in three sizes. The standard is 15 inches high. The miniature poodle stands 10 to 15 inches high, and the toy poodle is under 10 inches.

Schnauzers (SHNAUH-zuhrz) were once rat hunters and guard dogs. As family pets, they bring hours of energetic fun. Schnauzers come in three sizes from 12 to 26 inches tall. The usual color is a "pepper and salt," black and gray.

Toy Dogs

Pekingese

Toys are the smallest dogs. They are popular because they don't take up much room and are lively pets.

Shih Tzus (SHEED zooz) were once watchdogs for Chinese royalty. They were called Lion Dogs because of their long fur and brave spirit. Also from China are the long-haired Pekingese (PEE-kuhn-eez). Although small, they are not afraid of anything.

Toy Dogs

Franky Sue

Chihuahuas

Dachshund

Chihuahuas (chuh-WAH-wahz) are an ancient breed from Mexico. They are the smallest dogs. Some weigh under two pounds.

Yorkshire terriers (YAHRK-shir TER-ee-uhrz) are from England. They weigh up to seven pounds and have long, silky hair. They are also brave dogs.

Dachshunds (DOKS-huhntz) once hunted small animals called badgers. Their long bodies and short legs were a perfect fit for badger holes. Dachshunds have since become loving pets for many people.

Yorkshire Terrier ▶

Sammy

Unusual Dogs

Shar-Pei

Some dog breeds attract attention because they are different in some way from other dogs.

The large, furry chow chow (chauh-chauh) is different from other dogs in two ways. While most dogs have a pink tongue, the chow chow's tongue is blue-black. The chow's back legs are also completely straight. Most dogs' back legs curve out and then down.

The Shar-Pei (shayr-PAY) is from China. It looks like a little dog in a big dog's skin. Its soft skin falls in folds. The Shar-Pei also has a dark tongue.

The basenji (buh-SEN-jee) is one of the few dogs that comes from Africa. The basenji is different in that it never barks. It is also a very clean dog that licks itself like a cat.

Basenji

Dog Shows

Dog shows are held all over the country during the year. They are run by the American Kennel Club. Every show dog must have a paper that says it is a purebred.

People bring their dogs to a special ring. The dogs are judged on appearance and manners. In shows for working dogs, contests are held to judge dogs on intelligence and training. The winners receive ribbons, trophies, and sometimes money.

Mutts

Of course, no matter what breed it is, the best dog in the world is your dog. In fact, many of the smartest and most lovable family dogs are just mutts. Their parents and grandparents might come from many different breeds. But the background isn't important. What matters is the loyal friend, the wagging tail, and the cold, wet nose.